PRAISE FOR *ENJOY ME AMONG MY RUINS*

"Trust Juniper Fitzgerald to lead you through desert nights, early 2000s punk clubs, VIP rooms, childhood homes—and further, into a motley of emotion and memory. Fitzgerald knows complexity—and so she employs a mixture of the epistolary form, braided lyrical essay, allusion, stream-of-consciousness, and narrative storytelling. *Enjoy Me among My Ruins* revels in both experiential wisdom and craft."

—AMBER DAWN, author of *How Poetry Saved My Life: A Hustler's Memoir*

"*Enjoy Me among My Ruins* is a lavish masterpiece that pulses with savage and conceptual moments strung together by desire, motherhood, sex work, an array of strip-club creatures, and Fitzgerald's childhood obsession with Dr. Scully from *The X-Files*. Delightful and searing."

—ANTONIA CRANE, author of *Spent: A Memoir*

"Haunting and powerful, *Enjoy Me among My Ruins* traverses the American West and Midwest, conjuring the women and queers who have been forces in Fitzgerald's life, and asking them to come along on her journey to destroy the contradictions of heteropatriarchy and dance upon its grave."

—CHRIS BELCHER, author of *Pretty Baby: A Memoir*

"Juniper Fitzgerald captures so much of the feeling of the maternal erotic (re)productive body involved in the performance of sexual labor that is strangely (and erroneously) imagined to be

phenomenal, marvelous read

—@thot

T0017457

"*Enjoy Me among My Ruins* is ALL gorgeous, none of it reductive, on every page a phantasmagoric dreamscape, an herbal of nightmare plants, and a sharp-witted retort to those who would not suffer witches like us to live."

—CATY SIMON, coeditor of *Tits and Sass*

"Juniper Fitzgerald's story is atypical and anti-capitalist, mixing anecdotes from literature with letters from her childhood self to Gillian Anderson. Fitzgerald stands strong despite the way the world attempts to dim her light, criticizing her as a mother and dismissing her career. *Enjoy Me among My Ruins* is a brutal look at the world and a powerful story of survival."

—NIKITA IMAFIDON, Raven Book Store

"*Enjoy Me among My Ruins* weaves together streams of experience, exploration, nuance, rawness, trauma, and hope so fluidly that it becomes a powerful reminder of how interconnected they truly are. It is rare that we see a story of a mother, a sex worker, an academic, a vigilant survivor, an unbothered child ethnographer so seamlessly told in one breath. This book is the unvarnished poetry that we hope to write when we go to our journals."

**—KATE D'ADAMO, partner at
Reframe Health and Justice Collective**

"By mixing prose and poetry, theory and anecdote, Fitzgerald's style takes the reader on a wild journey through a critical analysis of the intersections of work, marginalization, and mothering."

**—ERIC SPRANKLE, professor of clinical psychology,
Minnesota State University, Mankato**

Enjoy me among my ruins

Juniper Fitzgerald

THE FEMINIST PRESS
AT THE CITY UNIVERSITY OF NEW YORK
NEW YORK CITY

Published in 2022 by the Feminist Press
at the City University of New York
The Graduate Center
365 Fifth Avenue, Suite 5406
New York, NY 10016

feministpress.org

First Feminist Press edition 2022

NEW YORK STATE OF OPPORTUNITY. | **Council on the Arts**

This book was made possible thanks to a grant from the New York State Council on the Arts with the support of the Governor and the New York State Legislature.

First printing July 2022

Cover design by Dana Li
Text design by Drew Stevens

Library of Congress Cataloging-in-Publication Data is available
for this title.

PRINTED IN THE UNITED STATES OF AMERICA

For Andi, mostly

A note: there is a dreamlike quality to exploring the past, a quality I have attempted to re-create here with a nonlinear, kaleidoscopic structure.

While writing this book, I often thought of the philosopher Ludwig Wittgenstein, who chose solitude because, for him, language was insufficient and limiting.

Alternatively, when asked about writing, Nabokov said in "The Art of Literature and Commonsense," *The pages are still blank, but there is a miraculous feeling of the words being there, written in invisible ink and clamoring to become visible.*

Language as limitation versus language as revelation.

And still others, like Maggie Nelson, experience writing and language as a kind of destruction: *Writing is . . . a* mordant *. . . it derives from* mordēre, to bite *. . . a* corrosive, she writes in *Bluets.*

Language as annihilation.

Peppered throughout this book are childhood journal entries—addressed to Gillian Anderson—as well as vignettes of the women who've shaped my adult life.

Language *is* limiting, however. I could never entirely write the queer love and tender spaces that I hold for other women, even as I paw at the revelations that such a love and space might render in the hearts of others. In these pages I am revealed to myself, too—my love of women started with Dr. Dana Scully from *The X-Files*; I now reproduce and cultivate that love in my material life.

Of course, the women profiled in this book are unfairly exhibited through the subjective lens of my memories; I have annihilated them in this way, a kind of mordēre.

Writing as love.

And love as bleakly corrosive.

Enjoy me
among
my ruins

"Time passes in moments . . . moments which, rushing past, define the path of a life just as surely as they lead towards its end. How rarely do we stop to examine that path, to see the reasons why all things happen, to consider whether the path we take in life is our own making or simply one into which we drift with eyes closed. But what if we could stop, pause to take stock of each precious moment before it passes? Might we then see the endless forks in the road that have shaped a life? And, seeing those choices, choose another path?"

—*Dana Scully*, The X-Files

Jean . . . .

I have tried and tried to add Jean to the story here, but every time I try to write her, I write her all wrong. I try to tell the story of her little bunnies, of living on Otoe Street next to the firehouse where she grows squash and peas. I try to tell the story of the perennially pink spaces that she occupies like a tattooed, drug-using Martha Stewart, spaces where she sews costumes that we slowly untie and take off onstage in the dank strip clubs where we work together.

I want to write about her brother, who is dying. And I want to write about how she cleaned his penis, once, when a sore exploded there, and how on account of his paralysis, he was unable to tend to it.

I want to tell the story of the man who raped her and how I punched him right in the fucking nose, then, exploding a balloon of blood and cartilage. I want to write about how he fell off his barstool and how I followed him into the alleyway with intentions of killing him.

I love her more than language can capture, and that is perhaps why I cannot write her.

"If I die before you, make sure there are cheeseballs at my funeral," I tell her.

1998, 13 years old

Dear You,

Hi. This is so weird. Like a new beginning. I never know how to start my new diaries. The reason I got you was because of the cover. It looked so awkward and unique and lost that it reminded me of myself.

My last diaries have been named Gillian. I say that I want to change the name every time, but I'm just too attached to Gillian. Like a comforting shoulder or something. So, Gillian you will be named, after my favorite actress, Gillian Anderson.

I love her so much. I want to meet her. I want to get out of this small town and meet her and finally start my life. I can't stand it here! No one gives a shit about anyone. Everything is like high school in that way—like, everyone worships Tony, the class clown, but he'll never care about anyone (particularly a girl) the way they care for him.

He's also the kind of guy that girls want to be seen crying by. They want to make him feel sorry for them and have him comfort them. But no matter how much attention you plan to soak up from getting people to feel sorry for you, it's just not worth it, considering that the other person doesn't give a shit. I know that's horrible and I would never tell anyone that because it's so scary. But no one on Earth gives a shit.

That's why I want to run away to New York City and meet Gillian Anderson and be free.

But sometimes I wonder if I will even live to see my sixteenth birthday. We bombed Iraq. On their holy day. We called it "Operation Desert Fox" because that's all this is for these people—a fucking "operation." And it's about to be the year 2000, possibly the end of the world.

One more thing, Gillian. I feel annoyed by everyone. I don't know why that was so important to write down, because as soon as I wrote it, I changed my mind, but I promised myself not to erase ANY split-second feeling.

Love,
Me

PS—My best friend Susie almost got raped. My mom says it's because she is a "Lolita."

1. Edits to a Previous Draft

At twenty years old, in a secrecy that makes the reproach more cutting, I let my liquidy insides patter onto pink tiles. It doesn't hurt at first. It never does.

When the pitter-pattering turns to swells of the stuff, spilling into the claw-foot tub in my broom closet–sized bathroom, I wrap the wound in toiletries and slip into the bed I've recently thrifted—the remnants of a toddler-sized bunk.

Miming Elisabetta Sirani's seventeenth-century portrait of Brutus's wife, *Portia Wounding Her Thigh*, the gesture is simple enough: I want to see how much I can take.

Nearly twenty years later, the spot on my skin is a constant reminder, a kind of prayer. It is impervious to freckles and sunspots, stitching a pale, linoleum-like scar the way one might wrap plastic over unused furniture.

This is what it is like to walk into a strip club: the cut of the spectacle is deep enough that initially the only thing you feel is the heat. If you can handle the dagger of it, the way it plunges through flesh and bone, there are scars and prayers to be had too.

— . —

I always thought that my story began and ended in strip clubs. I wanted to tell a flattened and titillating narrative about feverish movements through time on an impartial stage covered in glitter. I wanted to be *fun*, existing as a kind of cartoon in a commodified story about commodified blow jobs.

I wanted to distance myself from my muse, Nabokov's muse: *Lo, plain Lo, in the morning, standing four feet ten in one sock.* I was more like Dr. Dana Scully in *The X-Files*, I reasoned—ready to shoot a man in the dick simply for calling her "baby." In the mildly delusional insanity that comes with being a wide-eyed and obnoxiously optimistic hooker, I wrote that my power over men, like Scully's, came from a pistol at the ready, wherein my proverbial rod shot out "sex positivity" like a *Bang!* flag from a toy gun.

In an earlier version of this work, I told the story of Raven. All black-haired and leather-booted with bra straps in the pleated pattern of a pentagram; I am rather ashamed to say that all of her other features have since escaped my recollection.

I told the story of our stripteases inside a Nebraska club off Route 6 with raised wallpaper and red carpets, where framed flappers lumbered over our labor, preserved in the compliments of men. I told the story of fish scale. As if sticking things up my nose was the most interesting part of me.

In an earlier version of this work, I embraced a particular narrative the way a Wish Dragon squeezes into a teapot. But in so doing, I further (and falsely) dichotomized all of the Lolitas and all of the Dana Scullys of the world.

The truth is, as it were, *out there*.

But it's a little more complicated than that.

— . —

In 2013 I learned of my pregnancy while attending graduate school and working as a sex worker in Las Vegas, Nevada. My red bob and blunt bangs sprouted thicker, more luxurious locks, filling in the spaces where my mane had been manhandled by my drunk and high partner in the name of some illustrious anti-vanity project.

I sold pictures of my swollen feet to bonered men and as my belly grew, so, too, did my tits. Upon moving back to my hometown, I attempted to peddle my breast milk as a fetish ware. No sooner had I hit the "post" button, however, than my morally superior Midwestern peers booted me from the infamous bowels of Craigslist.

Shortly thereafter, I found myself on the set of a porno, negotiating the legal terms around the wheres and the whens of breastfeeding on set.

After a divorce and a doctorate, a global pandemic and a murder, after a smattering of death threats, a lot of books, and even more booze, I found myself offering up my past with a kind of addict's dissociation.

So I revised and rewrote and ambled out of the tombs of generational addiction just in time to hop right back in with the enthusiasm of a deeply deranged asshole.

These are my edits to a previous draft.

Cassandra . . . .

She is my friend. And I love her.

She gives birth to her babies in a kiddie pool in her kitchen; her friends help catch the newborns that swim out of her body and onto her breast.

The first time I ever see her, she is a blushed blur of maroon fabrics, thrashing in the currents of a mother's mourning. She wails from the side of the road while onlookers try to hold her back from bearing witness to the carnage the crash has wreaked on her child.

I stop to help, but when I look at the child, she opens her eyes wide and is suddenly, somehow, *my* child. I stumble back onto the hot ground; for years to come, I will see my child's eyes in hers.

After the crash that nearly kills her baby, our children become friends, running in the open spaces of rolling prairie hills. And later, when my own family threatens to kill me, my child and I will hide out on her farm in the middle of nowhere. She will nurse me back to health with herbs and farm-fresh meals, and she will teach me how to spot poisonous plants.

We will sip tequila in the twilight of slow-moving sunsets and fantasize about hemlock and justice.

I plant a catalpa tree in our front yard in honor of her child.

1997, 13 years old

Dear Gillian,

Today Greg asked me to have sex with him. Then he said, "You have a nice body and legs and I want to lick them." Greg is always checking me out. He looks at my tits. He stares at my legs and asks me if I shave. He's always asking how far I've gone and says I'd be real good at blow jobs because of my bottom lip.

Then all these popular guys came up to me and this one guy, Tesmer, put his arm around me and everyone started laughing and said, "How much did you get paid to do that, Tesmer?" and he yelled back, "THREE BUCKS!" Then his other friend said, "Come on guys, let's go rape Amber."

Life's weird.

2. Dead Bugs

There I am—little-girl me—in fuzzy kitty sweaters, tucked away in suburbia under a ceiling of glow-in-the-dark stars painted by women in sweatshops somewhere in the Global South. Having cybersex with anonymous people on dial-up, AOL internet is how I conceptualize freedom. That, and Gothic narratives.

Lucy in *Dracula*.

Dolores in *Lolita*.

Cynda in *Look for Me by Moonlight*.

Meticulously studying the way that women and girls in Gothic narratives are consumed by their own bespoke Humbert Humberts feels exhilarating. I study their every wrong move if only to imagine myself making better choices. And through them, I also come to fetishize violence against my own body. The unquenchable thirst of a man's desire comes to feel like the greatest compliment, and so I will seek out this feeling in my laundry list of lovers to come.

In Mary Downing Hahn's thirsty young-adult Gothic novel *Look for Me by Moonlight*, Vincent—the poetry-writing, smooth-talking vampire—seduces Cynda in much the same way that Dracula and Humbert Humbert beguile their bedfellows. But where Lucy and Lolita get devoured, Cynda—my Cynda—makes it out alive.

Mostly.

"I can see your nipples," my mother says of my prepubescent body.

The purple prairie sky illuminates my body in the spaces where my mother and I perform our nightly tragicomedies. She accuses me—and my nipples—of attracting too much attention. A hound to the stench of cigarettes to boot—her Virginia Slims, kept in the freezer—she also wonders aloud why I insist on pantomiming adulthood.

The answer, of course, is that I have my own array of Draculas and Humbert Humberts and Vincents: a happily married neighbor who attends church regularly, a dance instructor, a nanny, a collection of boyfriends, and even an uncle.

It's probably my nipples, I tell myself.

— . —

Beginnings are so damned hard, Vincent tells Cynda one evening as they converse about his writing process. *And then you get to the middle. After that, you have to face the end.*

My Vincent writes verbose tomes on a philosopher I claim to hate. It is important to disagree with him, sometimes, so that he won't think me just a rotting lump of flesh.

My Vincent knocks me up in the warehouse where we live. We bathe in a mop bucket with a hose he's jerry-rigged to the drop ceiling.

And my abortion goes all awry and my skin turns the color of ash.

Cynda doesn't yet realize that when Vincent speaks of his writing, he is really just gesturing toward the pieces of her that he'll devour: the beginning, the middle, and the end.

— · —

I meet my Humbert Humbert on the prairie. We paw at each other in the rancid back alleys of punk clubs on Leavenworth Street in the early 2000s, on soil poisoned by the ASARCO lead refinery. We share cigarettes with sex workers on the corner and I tell them that I think they're pretty. I start starving myself by eating one package of M&M's a day, buoyed by the high of caffeine pills, which I crush and snort in the bathrooms of Village Inns.

My Humbert Humbert says, "Cats are better than dogs, because dogs will eat themselves to death."

He gnaws on my flesh.

We have sex in an abandoned house and then, later, we find a cheap apartment with stained carpets off the interstate. My Humbert Humbert gives me little things. Pills. Cigarettes. Money. He fucks me with an empty wine bottle just to see.

He tells me that he got an erection holding his newborn niece.

He says that his favorite graphic novel has this little kid who tells his father that he's going to hump him.

"It is the sweetest thing," he says, caressing the space between his heart and belly button.

Years after I meet my Humbert Humbert, I suck a man's dick in San Francisco for two hundred dollars while he does that same thing—petting that small, open space on his own skin. And for some reason, it makes me vomit, thinking of my Humbert Humbert while I have another man's dick in my mouth.

— . —

My Dracula in the sex industry is a clammy undertaker who smells of something like formaldehyde. He shows up to the strip club around midnight every night and says, "Good morning, gorgeous."

And every night I pretend to be his menstruating mother.

"You frame the bloodied sheets for me to hang in our family home," he croons.

— . —

What I remember most, now, are the bugs. Those dead, scorched things in a velvet coffin.

The long, spackled corridor to my caretaker's room—my caretaker a man hired by my father's ill-fated lover, an arrangement that engendered a brief encounter with upper-class luxuries—is littered with my father's oil paintings. Portraits of naked women, disembodied vulvas, headless tits, mountains of dicks.

My caretaker, Sean, is naked on his bed like a Michelangelo marred in the emptiness of contemporary culture, mastur-bating to a VHS porn. I am only eleven, but he invites me to join the enterprise. When the protagonist of the '90s porn comes onto the face of his heroine, I recoil and asked if he's just pissed on her.

My caretaker's gratuitous laughter at my sexual naivete is followed by his setting fire to the monstrous desert roaches and their generations of offspring that reside in the foundation of the house. He wants to show me that he can kill things. Like a postcoital cigarette, Sean will continue his habit of harming other living things after sexually abusing me.

One afternoon, I collect all of the things Sean has killed and preserve them in a beautiful purple pouch: a "velvet coffin," I come to call it. And when my live-in nanny is unresponsively high, flirting with the sweet hereafter, I have my revenge.

I scramble to think of the ways that I might reclaim what has happened to me—the come, then the burning. I collect the pile of dead insects, a symphony of shame; I am determined to make this *his* shame, not mine. So I stuff his pants full of dead, crispy bugs.

It is the bravest thing I have ever done.

— . —

My Vincent looks old now. That thinning hair.

I give him eggs from the chickens I raise. "Delicious," he says. "Like duck eggs."

And I remember everything that only he could have taught me. Duck eggs. The difference between "sediment" and "sentiment." Kant. I compare these things now to other things that only my child could teach me. Tardigrades. Taylor Swift. The shape of the universe.

My Vincent drank me in—his Cynda—until he had his fill, leaving me tethered in the shadows of his satiated appetite. And even now I have difficulty understanding this as something other than romance.

—— · ——

Soused up, wearing a crop top and unironic mom jeans, I find my Humbert Humbert at the ATM. I've gotten a sitter for my child so as to embarrassingly exist in anachronism, letting my tired head fall in violent whooshes, only to pull it back up again and let it drop, marrying the top of my body with whatever drunken beat I think I hear in the heavy-metal band playing onstage.

The musicians are men I've known for decades. White and cis, they scream until they go hoarse. If it weren't for my saucy state, I'd feel deeply subjugated by my surroundings.

"Am I too old for this outfit?" I ask my Humbert Humbert.

But the power dynamics are all off. I'm much too hefty, with a constellation of wrinkles, to revel in whatever insult I've invited.

"Yeah," he says. "I mean . . . a crop top?"

I wander off, salty.

Peckish for trouble, I eventually peek through the unlocked bathroom door of the bar to find him sticking cocaine up the barely legal ass of one of my students.

And I drink until it hurts, until it feels like bondage, or like a wine bottle up my cunt.

I drink until I can convincingly blame my subjugation on others.

— . —

My Dracula is dead now. At least, that's what I tell myself. I tell myself that he died of overindulgence. In tranquilizing self-deception, I drink myself into hopeful stupors, assured that I will finally be relieved of his orchestrated folly.

Other times, the space around him is warm and soft; he fades into other clients, clients for whom my feelings volley from one end of the emotional spectrum to the other, often on a dime. I am convinced that anyone can love anyone else with enough cocaine.

The deliciousness of being pulled onto an erection can shift meaning in time; it can feel much like brandishing a powerful tool at one end of the space-time continuum, while feeling quite alien at the other.

I'm sure that many of my Draculas are still alive, actually. But I like to keep them tucked away in the crosshairs of delusion and desire, like yellowing Polaroids stuffed into the secret crevices of ballerina music boxes.

— . —

Using the same vigor with which I collect dead bugs, I transubstantiate into hawkeyed fascination for Draculas and Humbert Humberts and Vincents. I recognize this as the often heartlessly mocked stereotype of an abused little girl seeking refuge in other abusive places and partners.

"You're looking for a dad," my mother will eventually say before excommunicating herself from me for seven years. She does not intend to be heartless, I don't think; she merely wishes to save me from her own heartache. And perhaps, I think, I should offer that kind of grace to trolls on the internet plagued with an obsession for women with "daddy issues."

I come to learn the specifics of my mother's heartache as an adult.

— . —

Age three, tucked inside a beige house with altars to the Virgin Mary, there is a magnolia tree outside my window, bursting with pink buds as if an artist forcefully squeezed rosy paint from a tube. It is here, on Center Street, that my father learns of my mother's infidelities.

Out of spite or something similarly sinister, he attempts to kidnap me.

The judge acknowledges the failed abduction but deems the act more apocryphal evidence of parental unfitness than adultery; my father is awarded sole custody. It takes only three months for him to relinquish his parental rights entirely, and I move back in with my mother.

Like Dorothy Dinnerstein in *The Mermaid and the Minotaur*, I will come to resent my mother because of her omnipresence; I will come to see fault in her ostensibly duplicitous femininities. I will come to fetishize my father because of his ephemerality and because of his privileged ability to categorize women. If my mother can only point to my prepubescent nipples in shame, my father can, through his absence and treatment of other women, help me learn the utility of my body under heteropatriarchal capitalism.

My mother can only remorsefully lament her own proverbial dead bugs while my father holds the godlike power of labeling the things that hurt me, which feels more freeing than facing the throbbing pain myself.

For my mother—and many women like her—sex work, and the antecedent abuses that allegedly engender it, is a kind of adultery; she is uprooted by this, triggered to the nuclei of her cells in being forced to see herself in her daughter.

My Draculas and Humbert Humberts and Vincents are all scorched in their own perfect ways, like folklores that subsist by feeding on the vital essence of the living. In the boondock backwoods of fantasy, I build castles in the air, my own bespoke cottage industry of revised narratives.

Just as Cynda is eventually forced to grapple with the ways that she has been duped, existing in perpetuity in the dossiers of men, my mother and I start to revise our narratives of each other too. And in so doing, we both make it out alive.

Mostly.

Grandma . . . .

When she takes her young children, including my mother, to her sister's house in the woods of Appalachia, she discovers a massacre of flesh and rope. Her sister has tied her seven children to trees, leaving them to gnaw themselves free or expire trying.

When my grandmother is dying, she hallucinates that she is back in "them woods," those terrifying, timbered parts of her childhood that caused such a fright; she howls and turns a pale purple. A nebulous blackness, a singularity of Appalachia.

She is not as afraid in my arms. And in her final days, I crawl into her bed and hold her like a child. I read her *Moby-Dick* in between lines of cocaine and Valium in the evenings.

When she dies, she appears in my Las Vegas bedroom to ask what happened. And I tell her that she is dead. And she disappears forever.

1997, 13 years old

Dear Gillian,

So many sad stories. Michelle has to go into foster care because her dad beats her and her mom wants nothing to do with her. WHAT IS IT WITH MOMS? None of them seem to care about their kids.

Two boys at school committed suicide. One tied a chain around his neck, hung it from the ceiling, and stood on a chair. His mom came home and found him dead. This other kid killed himself trying to get air drunk.

And then I went to a party and Ashley and Kristine were bawling because they want to commit suicide too. And then Ashley started cutting herself.

Help us.

This isn't even my life. It's someone else's. Someone stupid. I want a new life, an exciting one. Not a sad one.

What if I end up becoming a hooker for the excitement? Probably not. Maybe not. Hopefully not. But I do wonder if I would like a life like that.

3. Fleur-di-lezzie

The stunted stillness to the blizzard months of the Midwest makes for excellent fantasizing. The way time skirts over the ice in hollowed strokes, flanked by the gray ghosts of the past and future simultaneously—it all feels like a momentary paralysis, like being coerced by the elements into a kind of presence.

When I was a little girl, I would lie in the cold of it all, as the fluttering flakes kissed my eyelashes. Then they'd turn a more ominous sludge of half-frozen, half-watery glop, like a potentially lethal slime careening down my temple. I'd wonder how long I needed to lie there before it all turned to heat, the way freezing-to-death bodies often experience subzero temperatures.

At the time, a woman down the street from me froze to death. A portrait—nay, a *warning*—of feminine indulgence and unpredictability; it was stressed, then, that she had indeed been drunk, and yes, she'd removed all of her clothing before shawling herself in the ice, an untimely and unfortunate death caused, as everyone agreed, by the cavalier ways she often handled her own body.

I like this plane of existence, this space that's so cold it loops back to heat, a space of agency and largeness, a space of unapologetic excess. And most of all, I like other women who flirt with existing there too.

— . —

Her legs are sprawled, the harsh stage light casting shadows in the dimples of her thighs as she presses a Hitachi against her clit. In the seconds before she orgasms, the feminist porn director yells "cut!" and the performer moans.

"I was just about to come!" she protests, and rolls over onto a pillow to finish herself off while the rest of us discuss the shoot. I excuse myself for a bodily need of my own.

My throbbing tits are an almost psychic siren call from the body of my babe. My gorgeous newborn—that precious and precocious thing that entered this world without breath, this magical animal that is my heart and my love—cries for me in the adjoining room, swaddled in the arms of her father. Surprising no one (but perhaps no less psychotically puritanical), it is illegal to breastfeed on the set of a pornographic film. And so, as I capture gyrating women on camera in one room, I pull down the collar of my dress, letting my engorged breasts fall into the mouth of my babe, in another.

The codified physical separation between bodies as makers of life and bodies as makers of orgasm is not lost on the rest of the crew. When I return from breastfeeding, I am weary-eyed and emotional and the collection of queers and misfits and sex workers—later, we will be known as the creators of the lesbian art porn, "Fleur-di-lezzie"—allow their bodies to fall to the floor, circling me, an invitation for healing. Apparently, I'd not hidden my postpartum depression and absolute exhaustion with social constructions of the Madonna-Whore Complex as well as I had thought.

"I'm sure you know, mama, but umm . . ." Holly says. She is a well-known performer in the industry, with strawberry hair and pale skin. She smooths out the printed poppies on her vintage dress before continuing. "People were not nice to me when I had my first baby, ya know?" She giggles uncomfortably, looking to the floor for answers. "They thought that I was harming my child just by being in porn. I can't . . . I can't even really talk about it."

"Same," says another, her dark hair tied atop her head in a messy bun, the earthy smells of patchouli wafting around her. "When I was moonlighting . . . you know, doing full-service stuff . . . clients wanted me to make one tit for them and one tit for the baby because they, like, didn't want to feel like they were sexualizing my kid or something."

"That's . . . not really how breastfeeding works," I offer, shyly and mournfully. We all shake our heads.

A petite woman with a blunt face, the faint yellow of her pleated pants dancing in the foggy sunlight, paws at her open-mouthed girlfriend. Her girlfriend holds her close, comfortingly, as she says, "I couldn't work at the brothels when I was pregnant because they said, 'Any man who'd fuck a pregnant person is a pedophile.'" Her girlfriend strokes her face.

We all take a deep, grieving breath before setting the scene again. A commanding butch dyke, whom I'd secretly crushed on for the duration of our work together on "Fleur-di-lezzie," wraps her arms around me and says, "It'll be okay, darlin'. I think you just need to get out of Nebraska." And I break into a soulful weep, being seen this way.

"Okay!" says Holly, clasping her hands. "Time to make some radical porn!"

We all wipe the tears from our cheeks, cocooned together against the harsh realities of a society that despises us with such ferocity that even little children joke about our deaths: *How many dead hookers does it take to change a lightbulb?*

When the wife-and-mother class is *also* the whore class, patriarchal domination is so threatened, so ultimately blanched and blinded by its own precarious ideology, that it digs its claws in deeper, threatening not only the safety of sex workers but of our children as well. As Pat Califia identifies in *Whoring in Utopia*: *The wife-and-mother class is not supposed to acknowledge the existence of the whore class because that would destroy the "good" woman's illusion [of a] faithful, loving husband.*

And so those of us who occupy these two classes simultaneously, those of us who must mourn the stigma and violence against sex workers on a daily basis, will continue to push back with images of lilies, of the fleur-de-lis, reclaimed and reimagined as *both* Madonna and whore.

— · —

The darkly humorous poetics of the universe are such that I no longer find myself craving snow. I frequently laugh at the contradiction—when my body clocked years of existence remaining within it, my mind longed for paralysis. And now that the body is slowing, time moving in large, heavy swaths, I want to circle back to the moment of birth, the moment of Spring's first betrothals.

First the tulips and then the daffodils, rejoicing in the barely unfrozen soil. Then the pink and red yarrow—A*chillea millefolium*, named after Achilles, who healed his men with the plant in *The Iliad*—followed by the yellow poppies and their delicate faces that hide in the moon's presence. My favorite, however, is the coneflower and her rooty foundation. That's what makes prairie plants so unique: their roots are longer, heartier, and more tenacious than most other wildflowers.

And who could forget the conjugal seduction of pumpkin blossoms, with their creamy insides like nature's cum and the prickly stems that protect them from the ravenous curiosities of raccoons and wild dogs?

Indeed, I will always appreciate the planes of existence where frost turns to heat. The best people in the world are the ones who bear the burden of this kind of presence, who carry the weight of it for so long, it requires nakedness in every sense of the word.

As for me, though, the cold and presence are a younger and healthier person's plane. So instead, I'm trying, as best as I can, to imagine my rebirth through the rapidly thawing earth.

She lives in a nineteenth-century brick building with a dumbwaiter that reaches into the scary parts of the house. Her frozen placentas lie bagged in the kitchen.

On nights when we drink too much, we get in bed together.

Her ex-husband is awarded sole custody of their children and she cannot mentally recover.

She joins a cult and disappears into a world of golden wormholes and magic rocks and vibrations that make you immune to rabies.

I call her, sometimes, when it's dark where I am and morning where she is. And there is a sense that she is still there, under it all.

I go to see her daughter perform poetry. Her daughter, onstage in the solitude of her mind, dressed in a pretty white summer dress, calls her mother a "transient hobo" in front of an audience that snaps.

And I see so clearly the havoc a man can wreak.

1997, 13 years old

Dear Gillian,

I wish my dance teacher would keep his filthy hands off of me! Just the thought of him makes me want to puke! It's all so sick and gross and filthy and scummy. I know what's happening with me and the dance teacher is happening with other girls. The touching is only the start. And I don't know why, maybe I was the lucky winner, but he's always falling on top of me. Two weeks in a row now. And once while he was on top of me he stuck his hands up my shorts.

Of course he tells me I'm the one doing it wrong, and I play fucking stupid and apologize. You don't know how hard it is to write down all this shit, but it's getting all too disgusting for me.

Then, we had observation week where all our parents came to watch and of course he kept his hands off of me. But after dance, everyone kinda huddled together at the front of the dance studio and I went to the back where no one could see me so I could put my cover-up on over my leotard—which by the way, shows how fat I am—anyway, I'm getting all my stuff on and look over to see perv boy staring at me. I act casually and say, "I'll get my back handspring next time." He comes over and tells me I already have them. And he just keeps staring at me. Looking at me up and down. And then he asked me if I wanted a ride home.

4. Dear [Redacted]

Last night I dreamed that you, my child, were a stripper. You were of age, of course, and I was much older. But I, too, was a stripper. Still. And in the style of my true nature, I stole money from you. In the dream, you were a young thing like I used to be, mopping up cash on the stage like a pro. You knew I'd stolen from you, but you felt sorry for me and ignored it.

It seems fitting that today, in waking life, I did indeed steal money from you. You are five—almost six—and I'm out of money until Friday. You had five dollars in your piggy bank, which I took to buy a cup of coffee. I stole a roll of toilet paper from the bathroom of the café and used the rest of the cash to buy gas. But just so you know, I put an IOU in your pink piggy. I promise I'll pay you back.

A whole year has passed since I first started this letter. You were turning six when the pandemic began. You just turned seven. And to tell you the truth, I've made a rather unsavory habit of dipping into your piggy bank. Sometimes just to buy cigarettes. I think you probably know this, and I'm sorry. You've taken to breaking apart the geodes that I bought you for Christmas in order to sell the tiny crystals from its insides to the neighbors for a dollar. It's like you're already giving up the things you love to protect me, and I'm just really sorry.

Last week, I took you dumpster diving. We scored a bunch of building materials and I transformed them into a bonfire for your birthday party.

We have our own Morse code—if I squeeze your hand three times, it means "I love you." And you squeeze mine back four times—"I love you too."

Squeeze, squeeze, squeeze.

I love you.

— . —

You have started playing chess. You've removed many of the pieces and replaced them with clay sculptures you've made: a dragon, a rainbow, and even seaweed. Sometimes I fantasize that Gillian Anderson comes to our home to see you play chess. There is part of me that would feel embarrassed with something like that happening. Embarrassed only because you are so remarkable, and your brilliance is desperately out of place here. Gillian would have to traverse a street full of broken bottles and houses where T-shirts serve as window coverings; she'd have to step over all the chicken shit in our yard just to see you play chess.

And I'm sorry about all of that too.

— . —

I was your age the first time a man sexually assaulted me. I was your age when I saw my beloved cat, Tabby, get thrown down a flight of stairs by a man who claimed to love my mother. His brutalizing the cat was my punishment. Then, a few days later, I came home to find that Tabby was gone.

I loved that cat more than anything.

These things are absolutely insane to revisit. I can hardly do so without falling apart. Indeed, I am falling apart. As I attempt to piece together this book, I am falling apart before your very eyes. We are late to school every day. Or at least, we were. When school was still being held in person. And now I'm stealing money from you. My five-year-old, six-year-old, now seven-year-old. Somehow, I am not as alarmed as one should be that I am, also, currently stealing toilet paper from local businesses until I get paid. I am not alarmed because this is how I've always lived. But I want you to know that this is not necessarily how I want *you* to live.

When I told you that I was almost done with my book, you asked me to take your name out of it.

"I don't want strangers to know about me," you said, and I felt that more strongly than you can ever know. Or I should say, more strongly than I *hope* you can ever know.

— . —

I recently wrote something about trafficking moral panics, and in the habit of our day, the publisher decided on a click-baity title about "the myth of sex trafficking." That's not what the article was about, but no one reads articles anymore, do they? People with money determine the discourse and the rest of us idiots fight it out like a real live *Hunger Games*.

Anyway, I have a lot of anonymous people online threatening to kill me, which is nothing new. But the most horrible comments are the ones suggesting that I am "grooming" you, my child, for the sex industry. That's a hard fucking thing to hear, let alone type out in a letter to you that, perhaps, I hope, you will never read anyway. There is quite literally nothing I can ever do to be seen as a "good mom" in this culture, and I hope that neither of us internalizes that.

I can scarcely witness you playfully wrestle with your own father without being triggered—a true, emotionally spiraling kind of triggered—and here I am, being accused of exactly what was done to me, exactly the thing that is inescapable, the thing that has truly fucked me up beyond repair.

I am told that my entry into the sex industry is because of my trauma. I am held accountable for that trauma, and when I attempt to make those conditions just slightly more bearable, I am accused of doling out the same kind of trauma onto you. It's almost like all of this is on purpose.

— · —

I'm not sure what makes a good mom. But I can promise you a few things:

First, if you ever told me that someone was harming you in any way, I promise to believe you and fight on your behalf. I will be accused of internalized whorephobia for feeling this way, but if a man ever fingered you at a bar and you were ambivalent about it because you never had the language to define what was happening, I would kill him.

Second, I promise to never verbally abuse you or harm the living things that you love. Somehow, fighting for sex workers' rights relates to all of that.

It's like this: Henri Lefebvre was asked if he was an anarchist. He said, "I'm a Marxist, of course, so that one day we can all be anarchists." Likewise, I am pro–sex workers' rights so that one day, no one will have to choose selling sex. I do not want you to be a sex worker, for fuck's sake.

The other night—in your strangely advanced philosophical way—you asked me if I'd be okay reliving my life. I shuddered. I don't want to redo any of this fucking shit. And in some ways, I think that is an admission—I don't want any of this shit to be different *for me*. Everything I've ever done led me to you. But that doesn't mean I want the same for you, and anyone who'd say otherwise likely has a trust fund.

My goal is to prepare you to be a person in the world without me.

It's okay if I die. It really is, my love. Even if I die in a super gnarly way like being dismembered by a lion.

Sometimes I think about how tragic it is that I'm going to die. I never felt that way before you came along. I've always been fine with my own death. But now, I know how much that would hurt you. I don't think I'm a great mom or anything like that, but I do know you love me. And I also know how devastating it is to lose the shit that you love.

I never had the childhood feeling of wanting to hold on to my parents. Both of them were so utterly detached from the beginning that, by the time I was your age, I was making my own breakfast each morning. And then when I got a little older, "breakfast" became a cigarette. I was just five or six years older than you are now when I started smoking regularly. I was twelve.

Sometimes I wonder if we'll die in some Lars von Trier–like catastrophe together, like in that movie *Melancholia*, in which case, lamenting my own death is moot. But let's say that doesn't happen. Let's say you survive this haunting of a world, this haunting I didn't know was a haunting until years after I decided to bring you into it. Let's say that happens.

Well, don't you ever forget that you are the most important thing to me, and fuck everyone else. Of course I hope you fall in love and all that shit, but no one—NO ONE—is better or more important than you. No one's needs or emotions are more urgent than yours. No one's trauma is an excuse to hurt you. Obviously, the opposite is true, too—you should never hurt anyone because of your trauma. But I honestly care less about all that.

I also want to say that *people have to know that surviving is a collective will.*

I wrote a letter to you when I started graduate school in 2008. That was worlds ago. I wrote a letter about the collective sense of hope in our country at the time. I even put an American Spirit cigarette in a box for you, just in case the *you* of years later (I wouldn't be pregnant with you until six years after writing the letter) would be curious. I snagged a newspaper from my neighbor—Obama won, of course.

I spent that evening at home alone while my new graduate-student friends partied. I spent the evening home alone with *you*, in some sense. I was so overwhelmed with optimism then; I can still see myself in that drug-riddled apartment complex, rocking back and forth on a tweed couch that I bought from Goodwill with the help of your other sex-working aunt, Megan, blowing cigarette smoke through the window into the desert night. There were swaths of abandoned hotels and timeshares; eviction notices and property-condemnation warnings were as common as the daily mail.

When I wrote you that letter in 2008, at a time when I still claimed that childbirth was "the most oppressive thing a woman could do," my mother, your grandmother, hadn't spoken to me in years. I had told her, while chatting on the porch of my childhood home, that I was a stripper. She told me to "leave and never come back."

I washed my dishes before leaving.

And then I bought an eight ball. I lived in a warehouse.

— . —

Yesterday I got paid. I bought you a coloring book for three dollars that came with glitter and crayons, and I put a twenty-dollar bill in your piggy bank. I also bought wine. And whiskey.

I bought pizza and Burger King and doubled up on all of our medications in preparation for being quarantined because of the coronavirus. My asthma medication, which is likely just COPD medication at this point, is five hundred dollars out of pocket.

"Why do they make it so expensive to breathe?" I asked the Walgreens clerk. The better question is, perhaps, Why do I keep making it impossible for me to breathe?

"They gotta get their money too, I guess," she said. She didn't even make eye contact with me.

— . —

Today you opened an umbrella in the house. It almost knocked you down the narrow, hundred-year-old staircase to the basement, where you would have likely cracked your head wide open on the concrete platform.

"Use your head!" I said, and immediately regretted it.

Your eyes got all wet, the way they do when you're about to cry but you still want me to think that you are strong.

"When you say that to me," you said, "I think that you think I'm stupid."

You have such a way of disarming me, even though that is not your responsibility.

I kneeled down so that I could face you, intensely, and said, "That's not what 'use your head' means. 'Use your head' means that you are brilliant and that I want you to use that brilliance to be good to your body."

But what I really meant to say is that we can't handle any more bad luck.

I love you. And I always have. I loved you before the creation of the universe and I will love you after it is gone.

I would relive this life an infinite number of times just to be able to meet you again and again.

And if you think that's melodramatic in any way, then *good*—you're clearly more adjusted than I am.

Squeeze, squeeze, squeeze,

Mama

Diana . . . .

Pretty and unshaven, Diana lives in a trailer park in one of the many dusty collectives tucked away in the desert. She makes art out of headless Barbie dolls and her partner gets tickled by men for money; he will later die of a heroin overdose.

We shotgun beers and smoke cigarettes. Diana hangs her lingerie on the fence, offering lonely passersby the opportunity to own what she's worn.

She shits into paper bags and takes the bus to the Las Vegas Strip, paper bag in hand, where she meets anxious men. They cover themselves in her feces before attending weekend-long conferences on financial management and concrete.

Days after I give birth to my child, my partner's artist friends write to congratulate him. One—a local artist— includes a quote about feminine mimesis in art and compares it to the masculine production of original work. Quite a claim from the mouth of a man who has never created another unique human inside his own body.

I think of Diana's art, sometimes. I miss her headless Barbie dolls and dumpster-dived meals. I miss her real, original work, woven into the fabric of survival and necessity.

2006, 21 years old

Dear Gillian,

I sat with two wealthy guys from the South tonight. They do something with computers and outsourcing jobs. I sold one my underwear.

Apparently people bid for slots on Google. It's not like the most reputable source pops up when you search for shit, oh no, it's whichever company pays the most to come up. Fuckers.

Serenity and Jodie, sworn enemies. Verbal fights, etc., at the club. And then tonight Serenity introduced Jodie to some guys as her "best friend." Crazy place.

Serenity is twenty-six with an eight-year-old daughter and she says she's a strict, overprotective mom.

Jodie is twenty-nine with a boy and a girl. She speaks Spanish and has a strap-on. I told her I thought she was hot and she grabbed my cunt. I told her I was wet and she said she knew. She's so drop-dead gorgeous. She's the "type" of girl I'd see on the street and think, Okay, act feminine and talk about boys so she doesn't think you're a lesbian.

Joanie is uncomfortable when others joke about us being lesbians together.

Laura always tips me now. In the bathroom tonight, she called me her "girl" and her "sexy bitch." We exchanged I love yous and I thought I could actually, really fall in love with her.

Serenity said that since she started stripping, she's become into women. "Guys are pervs. I go home to my boyfriend and it's like, 'Don't touch me.' Oh yeah, we've had way less sex since I started here."

Serenity is so interested in what I study and the papers I write.

"So, you study sociopaths?" her boyfriend asked me.

"Ha, yeah . . ." I said. "YOU."

Serenity works as a bill collector during the day.

My bucktoothed regular came in tonight. While dancing for him, I looked in his eyes and had a moment of sad thoughts. I thought how painful it is for all of us to be alive. This regular has always seemed nerdy to me, but not tonight. Tonight, he talked about his father dying, his friends that got shot last week, his addiction to painkillers, and his rocky relationship with his mother. He hates his job at Walmart. When I first met him, he was in a suit and had just taken his mother out for dinner. I thought that he was a sheltered mama's boy then.

Todd came in. I told him, like I always do, that he's an asshole.

When I was onstage, I heard one of the dancers at the table next to me: "Yeah, but she's really nice."

I suddenly wondered if I was, like, an embarrassingly bad dancer or something.

Pap came back, again. Abnormal, again.

Dennis was in. I explained why I never answer his phone calls. As always, he grabbed at my cunt. Said he thought he scared the new girl by trying to stick his fingers in her pussy. He and his friends called me "naughty" and undid my top. I *laughed and gave them exceptionally hot lap dances to tease and regain power.*

I took my panties off and put them in Dennis's pocket after a hot conversation about sexual fantasies—his was of his employees and dominating them, mine of my boss at the coffee shop dominating me.

He said he was going to make his wife smell my panties and jerk off. I told him I wanted him to wear them.

5. The Tulip

> *A kind of thoughtful Hegelian synthesis*
> *linking up two dead women.*
> *—Vladimir Nabokov,* Lolita

Every love story is a ghost story. And mine begins with tulips.

There are billows of blue fabric, compressed and released in a liquescent illusion. The fabric brushes the rafters of the old place—built by the hands of a man who will later be my lover—and returns to Earth with draft-loving cobwebs.

I am a Dead Woman in the play *The Tulip*; I recite my lines, which are mostly Dutch poetry. I later whisper these lines into the ears of Las Vegas strip-club clients, convincing them that I am an "exotic" European transplant. I drunkenly shilly-shally from Dutch language to British and Irish accents, a kind of hilarious drag performance that could only ever seem natural in the spaces of sex work.

I move too slowly in *The Tulip* to be detected by the naked eye, so once I've reached the other side of the stage, the audience member thinks to herself, *Has she always been there?*

There is also a Little Girl in the play. The actress who plays her is all grown up now, a big star in New York.

In the play, the Little Girl dies by drowning. I am tasked with preparing her for the underworld with the help of two other Dead Women. The ocean is unaffected by other actors' pleas; it was the Girl's fate to meet a blue, watery death.

We all say obscure things that the Playwright writes for us. Things about seeds and vegetables and butt plugs.

We say, "Chop wood, carry water. We built a world, that world ended, and we helped to dissipate the rest. The stage is empty, the props are gone, the lights are out, and the actors have left." We break the fourth wall in this play about a war over flowers. Poetic histrionics: I don't even think the war ever really happened.

It prickles your skin, if you're open to the wildness of it all.

"These characters hold the power of prophetic ghosts," the local newspaper says of the play, "evoking the past while at the same time bracing with the possibilities that lie ahead."

— . —

Mustard-colored rays of sunlight drape the desert in a kind of slow-moving chrome the year the Joshua trees blossom with tufts of white petals.

And I am pregnant—an unexpected thing, which I learn of under a burning August sun. The soles of the Playwright's sandals—he is now my lover—melt on the Las Vegas terrain when he shuffles all hunched over like the weight of the world is only tolerable if you don't look at it.

I love this about the Playwright—his slow movements and dark hair. I think to myself, No one has ever kissed me in public before.

Enfolded in the waters of my womb, my baby shares a dream with me—infinite gradations of blue, the color that novelist Ronald Sukenick says is the color of time. The color with which Maggie Nelson is in love: *Blue is something of an ecstatic accident produced by void and fire*, she writes in *Bluets.*

But when my baby is born, she isn't crying. She isn't crying because she isn't breathing. She has nearly drowned in the ocean of my body.

My dead grandmother is there in the room; she is the only thing that I can see. That, and stark whiteness. And I sit with my grandmother for a century or two.

The Playwright holds my knees steady. He holds his breath, waiting for his child. But I don't remember any of that.

— · —

Onstage, the three Dead Women say, "Toasting spice seeds will intensify their flavor. Toss seeds into a dry frying pan for several seconds over moderate heat, until they brown or change color, like a miniature autumn. Collect them in tiny bags and hide them in waiting rooms and church confessionals.

"Salsify and its cousin, scorzonera, are carrot-shaped root vegetables with a pleasantly mild, almost sweet flavor, which tastes like nothing but itself and the breath of young girls singing.

"This offers them good protection from the severe cold but keeps them buried in darkness."

A beat.

"In my day, no one talked about butt plugs."

— · —

In rehearsal, the Playwright moves my body from one spot onstage to another. And I blush. I blush to be touched. I blush to be madly, secretly in love with him.

He wears overalls like he's working class, but his hands are too clean for all that. He smells like cloves and perspiration, and he's engaged to a blond actress who, as he says, "likes sex as much as me."

When he follows me back to my home in the desert, we get into bed together and never leave.

At least, not until he leaves me for the last time. But that's not until later.

His apartment is made for artists, in an old building with thin walls. Vaulted ceilings and the sound of cellos; we know, but scarcely care, that our neighbors can hear the sounds of whips and reeds each night. Wayward bats fly in, sometimes. And the Playwright writes poems about them.

"I want to fuck you on that rug, there," I say.

"There are seven rugs . . ." he says. With an ellipsis at the end.

Sometimes, when we are both high on meth, he drags me around, naked, by the hair. And I fucking love it.

Oh, the weight three dots can hold . . .

— . —

The Playwright gets me a butt plug for Christmas. When we divorce, I cannot find it anywhere. Perhaps he left it in someone else's ass.

The Playwright says, "Linearity seems, to me, to better fit with the physical. When it comes to the . . . abstract, say, then often, a cycle seems a more appropriate condition."

— . —

The young actress who plays the Little Girl is carried around the stage by men. Dead and floppy in a dress that is as much baptismal as it is conjugal, she learns quick that, as Poe writes in his essay "The Philosophy of Composition," *the death . . . of a beautiful woman is, unquestionably, the most poetical topic in the world.*

Meanwhile, I am drowning in an all-consuming imaginarium constructed just for nightmares of my future child's death. I start picking at my skin until it bleeds. I start cutting out chunks of my hair.

— . —

I am having hallucinations. The cells of plants in midair. Pulsing loops that get more violent as the hallucination progresses. Terrifying kaleidoscopes.

I get lost in stores. Sometimes, I have to sound out the words to children's books. I get pushed into MRIs and CAT scans, the insufferable pounding of the machines drowned out by Frank Sinatra ballads they play to distract me.

I am not sleeping. There is a pain in my head so pointed, it makes me vomit. I am reading the biography of a woman whose name I later forget. She defends the use of exclamation marks and screams "put me in the bathtub!" whenever she's about to lose her shit.

I publish a poem in *sea foam mag* about postpartum depression:

> *The woman does not speak for a decade. Humans are so*
> *   complex!*
> *Humans try hard—they just keep trying. The baby studies*
> *   rabbits on*
> *YouTube. Sometimes, the bunnies' pellets fall to the*
> *   kitchen floor and*
> *the woman sweeps them up in her hands. "More?" "Shoe?"*
> *   "Milk?"*
> *"Patriarchy?"*
>
> *The woman is a public woman and this brings great*
> *   sorrow, she*
> *imagines.*

The Playwright—that romantically unruly genius—leaves me for good. He moves in with another Dead Woman.

— . —

"Are you now or have you ever been a prostitute?" the custody lawyers ask.

— . —

We cover the Little Girl in tulips and gently waltz to the haunting lullabies from Swedish *fäbod*. The Playwright is called "brilliant."

Men with sticks bang on the front of the stage.

All of the Dead Women are always in the background. We have floaty arm things to emphasize fragility.

Dead Woman 1. Dead Woman 2. Dead Woman 3.

Which one was I, again?

— . —

After five years of divorce, the Playwright and I drunkenly wrap our arms around each other. Our child sleeps in the upstairs room where we once made love. It is a sad campaign, mostly. Like lulling a ghost out of an Acheron configuration. I leave his house with a sense of shame, like I'm looking for a part of my timeline rather than any one particular person.

I stumble into the Lyft and say nothing.

Because every love story is a ghost story. And mine begins with tulips.

Jennifer . . . .

The house on the prairie is timeworn. The hinges stick and moan; the weight of stories makes the foundation sink to one side.

There are so many women in the kitchen cooking. Their bodies, like the old house, are robust. They wear aprons of assorted colors. The tattered screen door sways with the prairie breeze.

I walk through the house and find dangerous little boys holding knives in the rafters, grinning as they wield their weapons. So I run to the basement and in it, I find pages and pages of my writing, reduced to single pieces of paper, a tornado of ink and pulp. When the papers settle, there is a tiny child crouched under the ruins of it all.

I offer my hand to the girl who is trembling, and I realize that the girl is me, buried under the truths I meticulously cataloged.

1998, 13 years old

Dear Gillian,

I can't drown out the pain. I can't stand my family or even my friends. I just want to be happy. God dammit, this world is a whore.

I just want to run, run, run forever and I want to save myself but the more I force a smile and the more I see everyone faking their smiles, I just want to kill myself. I WILL kill myself, oh yes, Gillian.

I never watched cartoons when I was little. They were too fake and too unrealistic. I thought they were cheesy and annoying and horrible and I wish I could just go do the kinds of things cartoons do—fly off a bridge. Fly to San Francisco or Chicago. Wouldn't that be wonderful? To actually just run away for once. Meet a girl like me who wants to love me back. Feel the wind on my face and realize that everyone and every damn thing that's hurt me so much is behind my back instead of right in front of my eyes.

I'm going to start calling this place "Suicide-a-ha" instead of "Omaha" because it makes me so insane.

6. Fabulous Las Vegas

A surging ocean of rosemary is the perfect complement to the fallows of the desert. Contradiction can often be its own kind of consistency; the savage landscape of the Mojave lends itself to an unwavering loyalty the way a cholla cactus protects the offspring of a cactus wren. Only in the desert—and particularly in Las Vegas—does it feel completely natural and guiltless to snort cocaine in solitude on the roof of an apartment building until the wide, crooked face of the sun shows its gaping, gaseous wounds.

I hop a few fences, emboldened by the high, and make my way to the university where I am a graduate student. I love the contradictions of the desert's early morning—the still-drunk bums on Maryland Parkway and on Paradise Ave, the omnipresent hustle of sewer-dwellers collecting unclaimed slot machine wins, the weary-eyed tourists anxious to escape after very nearly losing their minds to the succubus of Sin City, the showgirls sipping coffee at the local casino buffet, and the eager students, shuffling out of sunrise study sessions.

I love the hustle on Boulder Highway, split into two—the track for teenage runaways, mostly queers from Mormon families, and the other track, adult junkies. I love the way the Blue Angel towers over all of us in her disrepair. I love the postapocalyptic survival shop, just opening, where you can buy guns and beer and bear traps at six o'clock in the morning; I love the abandoned theater, all *Metropolis* in structure and narrative, where squatters and guerilla art converge.

I love that Las Vegas is known for her adult landscape, but in order to reach it, she'll make you cross old barren train tracks. She'll make you bear witness to the extreme poverty that accompanies conspicuous consumption. She'll make you drive through the desert where the US military hides weapons in concrete bunkers before you can get your dick wet. She'll fly drones overhead just to remind you of the American Dream.

I love that life flourishes here in the absence of all possibility. I love that Vegas is unapologetic.

It is rugged here, and uniquely American. Here she stands, in all of her glorious contradictions.

— . —

There is a body memory to backstages in strip clubs. The corridors are thick, like the tunnels connecting stage right and stage left in high school theaters, those infamous spaces where queer kids catch moments of unsurveilled intimacy or, at the very least, fleeting fantasies of a gayness unbridled by Midwestern brutality.

You run your hand across the bricks of the strip-club back-stage, steadying yourself, shaking swollen ankles crammed into seven-inch heels.

The scariest part isn't the undressing; it's the assessing of one's body as you wait in the wings to hear the name you've chosen—Jenny, Dotty, Hazel Lee, Juniper. I've never been a Chastity or a Bambi kind of girl.

The backstage corridors hang low, shadowed by peeling plaster. Some backstages are carpeted, causing lumps of maroon threads to pill up underneath platformed Lucite and vinyl. Your predecessor mops up her tip dollars on hands and knees.

These stages, all sticky with sweat and glimmering with glitter, tell the stories of labor.

I love that life flourishes here; I love that women with broken jaws and broken hearts, women whose spaces have been metaphorically, metaphysically, and literally gentrified, find their way here. I love that women with dicks, women with scars, women who love other women, and women who long for abundance learn quickly how to navigate contradiction.

I love that in the absence of all possibility, women in the sex industry demand to survive.

There are six hundred miles of flood channel in the Las Vegas Valley, many beneath the neon. In the monsoon months when the desert swells with rainwater, the tunnels fill up at a rate of one foot per minute with currents as fast as thirty miles per hour. That's when the bodies pile up outside the Imperial Palace and the Mirage. The gold facade of the buildings, much like the hypnotic reels of slot machines, demand that tourists engage in *faceless* and *endlessly self-evident* performance, as Jean Baudrillard wrote of postmodernity in his book *America*, in lieu of acknowledging what's under their feet.

The mouth of one such tunnel lies adjacent to the goatish gazes of selfie-snapping novices at the foot of the Welcome to Fabulous Las Vegas sign in Paradise, USA.

A Lord Byron quote welcomes weary-eyed junkies to the threshold: *What is Hope? nothing but the paint on the face of Existence; the least touch of Truth rubs it off, and then we see what a hollow-cheeked harlot we have got hold of.*

There's a woman there, underneath, who sections off her bedroom from the bathroom with towers of empty 40s. Her space is a nice, damp reprieve from the ever-increasing summer desert temps. There's almost something comforting in rejecting reality itself, which is, as Baudrillard writes in *Simulations, entirely impregnated by an aesthetic which is inseparable from its own structure . . . its own image.*

The "reality" of Las Vegas's aboveground is nothing if not an endless reproduction of its own image.

In the underground, we smoke cigarettes and joke about the innocuous shit that "normies" on the top care about. Mortgages. The newest cell phone. Green grass in the desert.

Some people shoot heroin and talk about seeing the heads of Afghani civilians getting blown off during their time fighting for Operation Enduring Freedom. One man is missing half of his face; no one likes George W.

A hollow-cheeked harlot, perhaps. Though I fail to see hopelessness here.

— . —

At twenty-four—in a homemade perm I'd managed to do in front of the cracked mirror inside our warehouse homestead, where my boss-lover and I bathed in mop buckets and spent our evenings high on whatever we could find, very nearly squatting if not for the unpretentious rent—I run away to the City of Sin. Alcoholics and drug addicts like to run from everything but our own demons, and what better place to exercise such a thing than in a city marked by vice.

It is 2008 and the city is both a timeshare ghost town and alive with simulated luxury. Foreclosure notices and condemnation yellow slips litter the gutters with fliers for "Girls 2 U" and others that boast mobile phlebotomists for the particularly gnarly hangover.

The Mexican men on the Strip make an art out of clicking and snapping playing cards with naked women on the front, attracting the attention of a certain kind of stumbling, hushed tourist. Sex workers on dinner dates are the only sane demographic here, sober and stoic in heels. Young women in bridal parties attempt to copycat the sex workers' stoicism, but their performances are always too shallow, too insecure. They stumble from sidewalks into streets like baby deer in heels, having never had the material reality of laboring in such impossible shoes.

I get a job stripping at a Pacific Islander club off the Strip. It's a dive, punctuated by men who bring in their own toiletries to mop up the viscera they spill into their hands. I spend most of my time on my knees, shoving my naked tits into slouching, drunk faces, because when I'm standing, my head nearly touches the popcorn ceiling of the stage.

The VIP is a cubicle lined with carpet, sweat soaked and reeking of mold. I get off work at seven a.m., at which point I drink a beer on my patio, pop a Valium, and sleep until noon. When I wake, I cook broccoli or eggplant in coconut milk and suck on my asthma inhaler before smoking a cigarette. Then I walk the windy mile to school, swallowing uppers by the handful until I'm back at work at eleven.

On good nights, I score dinner dates of my own, flirting my way into free limo rides and dinner. The cruel poetics of it all is that I get a glimpse into this life of simulated luxury—simulated by virtue of being entirely symbolic rather than material—even as I can't afford simple things like paying off my overdue library books.

Enjay is Hawaiian, and my favorite dancer. She is a contortionist onstage, does push-ups in a pretzel shape; and a friend off of it. She drives me home, sometimes, and we sit in her SUV smoking weed until we can't feel our bodies anymore. She has a pet monkey that shits into its own hand. Elisa is Samoan and smells like cotton candy. She does my hair for cheap, sewing in strands of synthetic stuff backstage where the walls weep with the insides of broken pipes. She is a grandmother. And one night, she pulls on the fat of my back and says, "You're gaining weight. You're pregnant." And I laugh and laugh until I seriously consider the possibility.

When I'm home and indulging my normal beer/Valium routine in the early morning, I puke it all back up on the concrete and realize that Elisa is right. I am pregnant. And my baby is already protecting herself from my demons.

This life is flourishing within me in the absence of all possibility.

Marita . . . .

We hold hands with bellies full of absinthe, poised to jump off Eiffel's Liberty Bridge in Budapest. A man speaking Hungarian and huffing the contents of a brown paper bag pulls us off the ledge; we both wince to think of it for twenty years henceforth.

In Olomouc, I drink until I stumble and she playfully demands "Děláš?" over and over: "The fuck you doing?"

I am a bridesmaid in her shotgun wedding, just as she is in mine. Suffering the constipations of pregnancy, she is bloated and uncomfortable until just minutes before she is slated to walk down the aisle. I hold her wedding dress over our heads as she takes a shit and the wedding planner says "There's no time! There's no time!" over and over outside the bathroom door.

She will later wake to her evangelical Christian husband raping a friend in the bed next to her.

And later, our children will sit on the carpeted floors of hotel rooms, making dolls together while we smoke cigarettes outside.

And she holds me. And I hold her.

1998, 14 years old

Dear Gillian,

I love that the characters in books will always be at the same place where you left them. I do wish, however, that all stories took place in winter.

Anyway, as much as I should be studying, I REALLY have to tell you stuff. I know this is stupid and I shouldn't make such a big deal about it, but I'm going to tell you, so you can know what SCUM men are. It was Halloween last night. I had red-vinyl pants on. I went over to our neighbors' house, the couple whose kids I babysit. I asked the dad to borrow some face paint. The mom, Cathy, went inside to get the paint. The dad, while Cathy was inside, stuck his hands in my pockets and pulled me close to him. He asked, "Are these real pockets?"

I started blushing and said, "Yep."

What the hell kind of question is that? But see, I don't think he meant anything sexual about it because my friend Sarah was standing right there and he wouldn't have done anything wrong with her standing there, right?

This is my opinion on the whole thing: I'm mad but it doesn't bother me. I'm being a drama queen. But I keep writing.

I need to stop being this stupid "victim" bitch and fix the situation. I think what I'll do is go over there when Cathy is gone and stick my hand in her husband's pocket and, in the most seductive voice, say, "And are these real pockets, baby?"

Fuck it. I'm going to bed. I love you, Gillian.

7. Swine on the Island of Aeaea

Witches are not so delicate.
　　　　　　　—Madeline Miller, Circe

The sharp-lettered "Dr." cuts through the red font of the services provided: humiliation, sissification, femdom, and all-around feminist bitch. I put piggy emojis in my text correspondence with men; the spells and potions of my labor turn men into swine. I lure and seduce and transform on my island of one.

My tits are a magnetic force of masochistic fantasies, spilling over the brim of my blazer, a voluptuous opium dream. I am one hundred pounds heavier than when I first entered the sex industry seventeen years ago; I have collected an assortment of charms.

My feminist texts are a kind of witch's familiar; I strike them with a heavy hand across the pale asses of men, my little pets. Actually, I strike them against my own thigh, leaving bruises, because my swine serve me—their benevolent dominatrix—over the phone.

In the icy-blue basement of the home I purchased with the contents of men's wallets, I assess my collection of rainbow dildos, vibrating butt plugs, and Hitachi magic wands. I scribble new ideas, new words, new narratives for the ways that I squash my foot into the snouts of my followers and the ways their muzzles hang on to its bridge.

"I start to lick up your leg, Mistress," Kenny says, "and I want to go further. Will you let me remove your panties, Mistress? *Will you?*"

I brew spells to keep my piggies on the line—not because I enjoy their company, but because I make a dollar for every minute I keep them ensnarled.

Sometimes, I read them entire books on feminist theory. I hear the faint *slish-sloshing* of cocks in the beats between Luce Irigaray's words from *Sharing the World*: *Our eyes are not capable of seeing, nor even contemplating, intimacy, at least not directly.*

But I do not mistake the incorporation of feminism into my sex work for liberation. This is merely one underpaid, shitty job in a long line of underpaid, shitty jobs. But "shitty job" is not the same thing as "sexual exploitation."

— · —

I am Circe on the Island of Aeaea.

Circe is a minor goddess in Greek mythology, often reduced to her elemental parts as a banished enchantress who ostensibly turns men into pigs for sport. Madeline Miller subverts the traditional telling of Circe's story in her novel *Circe*, suggesting that the spell for swine was born of necessity—after wayward shipmen repeatedly rape her, Circe transforms the men for her own protection.

Hers is not the story of exploitation or liberation, but one of survival and necessity. Men become pigs of their own volition and as a direct result of their own violence.

The minor goddess's conditions were dictated by the hot rays of a patriarch who wished her harm; her witchy brews were antidotes to patriarchal brutality.

Her labor was neither liberating nor exploitative; it was just *survival.*

And any moral or ethical argument that leverages the unsavory behavior of swine as tacit proof that those of us who service them simply shouldn't survive is not—or, *should not be*—feminist doctrine. It is, rather, bloated bigotry and concern dressed up in pompous language, peddling philosophy.

Deontological claims about the ethics of any one kind of labor, particularly labor that varies so extremely, like sex work, is unbearably lazy—*especially* when the claim focuses only on the variable of consumption. Consuming women hurts all women, the argument goes, and therefore sex work is universally unethical.

And while I have no interest in defending wayward shipmen, it's decidedly not my fault or the fault of any sex worker that sometimes our survival depends on the transformation of men into pigs.

— · —

"Do . . . do you really have a PhD?" my piggy stutters.

"Yes," I coo, and roll my eyes. "I really do hold a doctorate."

What I don't say is that academia necessitates my erotic labor too. What I don't say is that as an evergreen adjunct, my heady labor is far more precarious than the wares of my body. What I don't say is that there will always be far more men looking to be licked with a feminist text than students reeling to read it.

"Wha . . . what's our lesson today, Mistress?"

The scars on my swollen stomach pulse as if they might rip wide open. My body is wounded; several surgeries have punctured my flesh with a thousand sharp objects; I long for the comforts of bed.

I am made weary-eyed by the needs of the men who call my phone-sex line, even as I lasso them into lucrative conversations.

My client slips into exhausting exposition and I busy myself with fantasies of the past—how light I felt when unapologetically saying to my country friends, "I am a hooker now." How I felt like the moon's Mistress, free to move in and out of spaces in whatever ways pleased me, a pocket full of cash.

The sensation that liberation is the same thing as being wanted is a profoundly seductive narrative. Indeed, back when I was still skinny in pastel, I met women who were like me now. They were the cautionary stories of which I am now the star. My body is now both an apology and a warning.

At the time, I wanted my story to begin and end in the beds of my lovers, commercial and otherwise. I had fantasies of notching my skin the way a girl notches her bedpost, ticking off a laundry list of lays. I had hoped I'd be dead before I was gray.

I told myself I was powerful. I believed myself sexually liberated.

But really, Circe was not liberated—and to be fair, she was

not *not* liberated either, neither in the narratives that others tell of her nor in the witchcraft she cultivated.

— . —

My client's orgasm makes me inaudibly sigh. I turn my head up to the rafters where daddy longlegs congregate, cut off from the world of mortals. Part of the ceiling remains unkept, cracked and sunken in, the holes fossilized with webs from last fall like blueprints for newly hatched spiders. My piggies love sending me presents—corsets, high heels, lingerie. But never anything useful. Like plaster.

A beat. A yawn. I glance at my watch.

I endeavor to insult this man, to fuel his fantasies by hating him more even as he tops from the bottom like most insufferable het men do. Instead, a soothing, sexy voice cuts me off:

"The time allotted for this call has ended," the voice says.

"Goodbye."

I hang on the line to hear how much income I've generated from the exhausting masturbations of a man I don't know.

"This call lasted for sixty-three minutes and twenty seconds," the voice says, in a tone decidedly less sexy than her flirtatious goodbyes.

"You have earned sixty-three dollars and twenty cents for this call."

Sixty-three dollars and twenty cents will be an entire grocery bill for my child and me, provided I steal a few things like I always do. It never ceases to amaze me that some are able to spend what is for me grocery monies on something as simple as an orgasm.

Tonight, I think to myself, we shall have pork.

Anita . . . .

She is six months pregnant, nursing a beer at the dive bar where I work. She gives me all of her Girlfriend Experience clients now, on account of her pregnancy.

When a man rapes and murders a handful of sex workers, the news media interview her.

One interviewer vulgarly says, "You don't look like a sex worker. You look more like a librarian."

And Anita allows herself a beat before lacerating the interviewer with her wit and candor.

"How could that possibly be the thing you're thinking about when sex workers are dying?" she demands of the interviewer, unrhetorically. And the two of them sit in uncomfortable silence before the interviewer apologizes.

Our culture's obsession with sex workers lends itself to what Baudrillard critiqued as (embodied) simulation. That is, *women as the sexual scenario*, as he writes in *America*. Our deaths as sex workers are always second to the more pressing question of our fuckability.

Anita is the first person I tell that I am pregnant.

And she says, "You better make sure the Playwright won't take you to court for being a whore."

It was as if she knew then what I would only know later, which is that my labor in the sex industry will always be a barometer by which my maternal abilities are measured.

1999, 14 years old

Dear Gillian,

I talked to an enormously intelligent man at Grafieté, the goth store. We talked . . . well, actually, he talked . . . about history and how women were nothing then and how I should feel lucky now. He talked about a movie named Pi *and how math is the universal language and how if you figure out the code to every-thing mathematic, you will hear God. He made me feel so stupid. I thought I knew a lot and now I realize I don't. His intelligence was unhuman and I was so mad I couldn't match him!*

I wish I could have been dangerous to him. I don't mean dangerous in a bad way, I just wish he would have seen me as an equal. Or at least I wish that's how I would have seen myself.

Oh, and by the way, I'm going to be a famous actress like Gillian Anderson.

PS—Remind me to tell you about the little problem at the Cher and Cyndi Lauper concert.

8. Hemlock

Hemlock is a gorgeously symmetrical plant with leaves of lace so ornamental, its legacy in the canon of scandal feels histrionic upon first glance. But closer inspection reveals the warning emitted from its stem—a deep red stains its skin.

It is really quite something to stand in a field of the stuff and marvel at its delicate yet deadly enormity. There is a sense that Socrates himself haunts the prairie winds where the poison grows, "billowy" and reaching to the "brilliant sky" of Red Cloud, Nebraska, that Willa Cather observed in *My Ántonia*.

My child and I sleep on a blow-up mattress in the middle of a hemlock field. I note the poetics of it all; we are hiding from my family, who have threatened to kill me. They'd rather I die than reveal our hoarded family secrets of generational abuse, working-class white supremacy, and sexual violence.

Don't think that our silence means we've forgotten about you, the note in the package reads after I file a police report implicating all of them.

Love,
Your Family

— · —

Toxins are everywhere.

But in the evenings when the coyotes howl and the barn cats stalk field mice, my child dances arm in arm with other children under the orange glow of the moon. We are on a queer anarchist farm in the middle of nowhere, where the collective approach to child-rearing and other domestic tasks means that everyone learns quick how to outwit poison.

— · —

In "m/other ourselves: a Black queer genealogy for radical mothering," Alexis Pauline Gumbs writes that we can learn to mother ourselves because *love is possible even in a world that teaches us to hate ourselves and the selves we see waiting in each other.*

Queerness means surviving and escaping the spaces we were not meant to survive or escape. *To answer death with*

> *utopian futurity*, Gumbs writes, *is a queer thing to do . . . The radical potential of the word "mother" comes after the "m."*

— . —

All of us toy with our family loom, weaving knots of rage into generational sorrow. Some of us hurt ourselves. Some of us hurt others. All of that heaviness has to go *somewhere*, after all.

In my mind's eye, he is a sweet little boy, fighting back tears after I broke his glasses with a baseball. Then, he is yelling at us—the naughty younger cousins—because he's the oldest and we're ungrateful brats who've just been caught stealing, caught running away, caught smoking cigarettes, caught making mud pies. He yells because we should know better, because he knows what will happen if our fathers find out. He yells because it is better to be yelled at than to be whipped with a belt. He knows that last time, our sadistic punishment was to stand in a charcoal hallway, our eyes held open as our uncle plunged his dirt-covered fingernail into them. He knows that that could have blinded us. He knows the way our young bodies are owned by these men. And he knows that we are quickly collecting generational sorrows of our own.

In my mind's eye, he is still childlike, sitting there across the table, blushing as he explains that he met his partner at the strip club. A dancer, just like me.

And then, just like that, he broke. He cracked wide open, hurting himself with drink until that pain—the very pain I recognize in myself—spilled over into another's cup. He pulled a gun out on his pregnant partner, the one he'd blushed to introduce, and no one really knows what happened after that except that the mother of his unborn child took a sledgehammer to the house while my aunt, a nurse, tried to stitch her child's brains back into his skull. He turned the gun on himself, apparently.

At his funeral, I can't feel anything, so I take shots of whiskey until I do. His father grabs me hard and I start to weep. I start to weep because I am afraid of him, because I am afraid of myself too.

— . —

My uncle Victor is unrecognizable, standing there next to Michael Jackson. His arms are all snakish and twisted, his head is thrown back, and his mouth is open, hungry. Prosthetics raise the contours of his face, and his skin is blistering and peeling away in patches.

He escapes the brutality of our family.

He is kind to me; he runs—with a leap and a plié—from the crooked purple raisin–like faces of farmers who "beat the sissy" out of him to LA. By 1982, he dances with Michael Jackson in the music video for "Thriller."

He is a zombie in the video. A beautiful, perfect allegory for being HIV-positive in the 1980s, surviving the banal brutality of the Midwest alongside the fascist politics of the day. Like Susan Sontag's *AIDS and Its Metaphors.*

"It's because of the gay-related something or other," my family says in their Nebraska drawls in kitchens with duck-printed wallpaper and yellow accent pieces. "Because Victor is a faggot."

And I realize, then, that I am also this thing called "the Gay-Related Faggot."

When Victor dies, I am instructed to tell others that he died of pneumonia. I am instructed not to speak of his husband—his "friend"—John. And it is his "friend," another gay-related faggot, who will be one of my only allies when my child and I go into hiding.

Indeed, it is my faggotry—and the faggotry of others—that offers respite from my family loom and shelter from the generational sorrow that makes me both hate and fear myself.

It is the gay-related-other that will protect my child too.

— . —

In Rachel Cusk's memoir *Aftermath: On Marriage and Separation*, she writes, *The problem [of writing] usually lies in the relationship between the story and the truth.* I remember learning about the unfortunate souls who've had their right and left brains severed, and how the job of the left brain is to make sense of everything that's nonsensical. I often wonder if people with brain-severed bodies experience the "story" and the "truth" of their lives in two distinct ways, like parallel timelines tutting on simultaneously but never intersecting.

I ask myself, What is my truth? And what is my story?

— . —

Mornings in the Mojave are always vulnerable and exposed in ways that seem to contradict the necessary hardiness of surviving an impossible place. The sunrise is perfect and still, casting her light on a city that will soon become aggressive in all sorts of ways.

The guttural calls of hawks serenade the open desert, and beads of sweat pearl up on the brows of early-morning tourists.

Lovesick, shedding our clothes in hurried strips as the sun comes up, we land on her couch caked in the visceral smells of Vegas casinos. She is on top, a scenario I'd played out for years in the shadowy twilight of the bars we frequented, even when she had other women around her neck.

"Have you ever been fisted?" she asks.

I am clumsy with words, hands, touch, lips, tongues.

"Nuh—not really," I manage. She smiles and takes out a latex glove.

She is the person I think about when I sell sex, even now. It makes the enterprise far more enjoyable, imagining her wriggling there, atop the weight of my body. And I feel, for a moment in time, that like my uncle Victor, I am, at the very least, attempting to be *conscious* of the delicate yet deadly parts of my past.

— . —

In *Gothic Queer Culture: Marginalized Communities and the Ghosts of Insidious Trauma*, Laura Westengard writes that Gothic narrative reflects the *insidious trauma* of being marginalized as Other. She says that the *containment crypt* trope of classic Gothic texts as well as in more contemporary lesbian pulp fiction presents queer sex as *monstrous, abnormal, and pathological.*

But it is also precisely at this intersection of monstrosity, abnormality, and pathologicality where queer liberation lives: not poster children for homonormative narratives about fucking and consumption and property ownership and child-rearing. But instead, monsters with peeling flesh and scandalous bodies, helping one another navigate fields of hemlock under a harvest moon.

Dakota . . . .

She is on acid or ecstasy or a combination of the two. I am at the wheel, speeding toward a Colorado rave in a warehouse despite being too young to have a driver's license. We feel grown because we've just started the first Gay–Straight Alliance in Nebraska; we routinely receive death threats and are followed to our classes by security guards.

Acid and ecstasy and driving too young aren't much compared to our daily realities of high school.

Later, we both enter the sex industry.

Her straight job's boss rapes her but no one believes her because Dakota is a sex worker. Civilians often think that sex workers de facto harm ourselves, and so it is ostensibly nothing if not expected that we should be harmed.

She makes $300,000 in cryptocurrency in one day. And the first thing she buys is an enormous stuffed bunny for my child. And then she sends me money.

When she walks the red carpet of the Academy Awards of Porn, I show my child her picture.

"Wow!" my child says. "Aunt Dakota looks like a princess!"

And she is. She is my princess, my sober, strong queen. And I love her.

1998, 14 years old

Dear Gillian,

You know what the greatest thing would be? If I fell in love with someone who really cared. But let's face it, the only people who care about things are the gay ones! Maybe I'm a lesbian. I mean, girls can understand girls, right?

Why does love have to be such a complicated thing? Why does life have to be such a complicated thing?

I do think I'm bisexual.

Beth drove me home tonight from this Bible study group I joined. And there is something to that girl. There is something within her that is so intelligent and deep and hidden that I wanted to know everything inside her. We were driving home and it was pretty dark outside. The way she joked and the way she worded every sentence was such a turn-on. I wanted to kiss her right then and there. I didn't, though. I wonder why I didn't. I wish I had . . . What harm could come from a kiss?

My horoscope today said that Leos make good actors, lawyers, and writers, and also that we have probably been dreaming of our honeymoons forever.

I hate that, Gillian. I don't want my life to revolve around a stupid guy. It would be different if I could have a honeymoon with a woman. But it's all so hard since all I can think about is falling in love. I mean, truly falling in love. I want to be with someone who wants to be with me as much as I want to be with them and it just seems like those kinds of people aren't in Nebraska.

Tonight, my mom told me to make the sign of the cross at dinner as she said grace. When I refused, she said, "Please just let me die happy."

9. We Shall Be Monsters

It is true, we shall be monsters, cut off from
all the world; but on that account we shall be
more attached to one another.

> —*Mary Shelley*, Frankenstein;
> or, the Modern Prometheus

Purple-thistle hills and groves lined with coneflowers swallow up the horizon where abandoned concrete malls surrender to more contemporary open-air markets. Bodies shuffle with idle curiosity for fleeting pleasures, unfolding textiles and boorishly letting them drop back down again into a discarded lump, these cavalier handlers either ungrateful for or unaware of the labor of service workers. Sometimes, it's hard to tell where the concrete parking lot ends and the digits of these bodies begin.

An erect steeple towers over the open-air market, the way men here guard the private property of their daughters' bodies—all those concealed shotguns at proms or other coed events. Years ago, a nasty storm uprooted the spire and dropped it, needle nose-first, into the heart of the minister's car.

"God works in mysterious ways, I guess," I said then, addressing the car's massacre to no one in particular.

"Midwest nice" is the gurgling anger of truth under a bovine film of cordiality in Middle America; it's like we're white-knuckling pleasantries with the devotion of a 1950s housewife. If you forget your early-morning manners or divert your eyes from coerced interaction at all, you will find that you are fancied a monster by the same folks who gnash their yellowing werewolf teeth at the slightest inconvenience.

Beyond the coneflowers and bloodthirsty bell towers are quiet cul-de-sacs of suburbia where fathers slip into the moon-wet bedrooms of their daughters and spend Sunday mornings in gold-leafed churches alongside abused altar boys. My uncle sees a priest from our church in a turnstile years before the sweeping abuse trials, and through the thick glass, almost as if in slow motion, he says to him, "You're a motherfucking son of a bitch."

The Midwest, like Dr. Frankenstein, is a half-frozen muddied pool filled to the brim with grief, *a frightful fiend / Doth close behind [me] tread*, as Coleridge writes in "Rime of the Ancient Mariner," also quoted by Shelley in *Frankenstein*.

The middle of America is where priests stick hands up my matriarchs' skirts while my toddler of a mother cleans out ashtrays, her little baby fingers reaching into cat-litter sand, smelling of the stuff and of sour tobacco for hours to come.

When the wind blows west here, the air is saturated with feces from the stockyards, out of which cows eventually travel through underground tunnels to the slaughterhouse. I liken them to World War II soldiers in the warren underneath Arras, covered in shit. When the wind shifts east, it carries the sweet scent of cornflakes from the Kellogg's factory, with just the tiniest hint of toxins that seem to dull the senses ever so slightly. It smells like the Martha Gooch macaroni factory where my father works, cleaning out the flour-bin silos and often collapsing in exhaustion on the roof of the place. Sometimes, he works the factory line for Seal-Rite Windows, drilling one screw into the same place ad infinitum as a joystick cog.

There's the mansion erected in the 1980s, fashioned like a Trolley Era classic with materials that won't last as long, where my friend used to live. When his mother gets her nails pressed on at the only nail salon helmed by white women, she says, "My son's not gay, my son's not gay," to no one in particular. She doesn't believe in vaccines and recently purchased a town in western Nebraska for the sole purpose of hiding from the "tyranny" of public-health mandates. Not unlike Mary Shelley's father in Somers Town, fleeing the guillotine.

The post office got robbed a few years back and the long stretch of unadulterated prairie circumnavigates the post-office building and reaches from the farm that my grandparents tended—but did not own—called "Boys Town," all the way back up to the high school.

"Why are only boys allowed there?" my child asks when we drive past the sign. They can read at the age of five.

I think about the time my janitor grandfather minded Charles Manson on the grounds of Boys Town; Manson was just a troubled teen then. I think about how now, my own brother straps kids to their beds in this horror house of a robustly funded Christian organization.

I say, "People of all genders go there, my love, but it's not a very nice place."

Underneath it all, under the new construction and glitzy billboards purporting to "save children," is a ghost garden. Corn, beans, and squash. The Three Sisters support one another: The corn gives footing to the beanpoles, which in turn remove nitrogen from the air. The squash, in all her prickliness, ensures protection from predator paws and covers her sisters in a shady reprieve.

This is where the ghost of my grandmother lives, entangled in the vines of her ghost garden.

— . —

Prometheus gave fire to humanity and was punished eternally because of it.

In contemporary parlance, we tend to think (inaccurately) of Frankenstein's monster—not Frankenstein himself—as the modern Prometheus. But it is indeed the curious doctor—not his monster—who parallels Prometheus in Shelley's evergreen tale. This is a comforting reminder for me—that is, horror need not be punishment for ostensible transgressions like curiosity, but can be, instead, a tool for reflecting on trauma. *"Monster,"* Susan Stryker writes in "My Words to Victor Frankenstein above the Village of Chamounix," *is derived from the Latin noun monstrum, "divine portent," itself formed on the root of the verb monere, "to warn."* Stryker continues, *Monsters, like angels, functioned as messengers and heralds of the extraordinary. They served to announce impending revelation.*

Prior to publishing *Frankenstein*, Mary Shelley wrote to her friend, Thomas Jefferson Hogg:

> My dearest Hogg my baby is dead—will you come to see me as soon as you can—I wish to see you—It was perfectly well when I went to bed—I awoke in the night to give it suck it appeared to be *sleeping* so quietly that I would not awake it—it was dead then but we did not

find *that* out till morning—from its appear-
ance it evedently died of convulsions—

Will you come—you are so calm a creature
& [Percy] Shelley is afraid of a fever from the
milk—for I am no longer a mother now.

I think this is why I sympathize with Frankenstein's monster
and why, perhaps, I am somewhat unhealthily obsessed with
my own trauma. The monster is both sublime and vile,
sitting at the unbearable intersection of heartbreaking
contradiction. Sentient yet made of dead things, much like
Mary Shelley's breasts wept with milk even in the absence of
her child, he is both alive and dead, full of love and rage,
questioning the dichotomy of science and nature. He is the
pendulum of bespoke monsters even as his creator values
things I tend to covet, like curiosity and creation and
wonder.

— · —

On account of having no doors, one does not enter the
house, but rather materializes inside of it. Like any other
phantasmagoria might appear to a fevered mind, one is
compelled to ask, "Is this my nightmare or the house's?"

The muted purple acanthus print peels away from the calci-
mine and plaster; the cast-iron bed with a horsehair mattress
is pushed against the windowless wall in the bedroom without egress.

I do not see the garden or the storm outside, but I can feel them both.

Black lace trees with white blossoms and Sui dynasty–flowers get pummeled by the raging winds. There is a canopy of miner's lettuce and daffodils. A mackerel sky, pumpkin blossoms close up on their drunken pollinators. Fireworks fly from transistors across the city and sleepy boulders rest on the tops of cars. Uprooted telephone poles make dams of debris in the centers of roads, and I hear my chickens cackle in the muddied backyard.

In my waking life, when I am not trapped inside this house, I dig trenches for cracked corn; it keeps the chickens alive in negative-forty-degree windchills. My child and I plant sunflowers that tower over our house and our pumpkins sprout from compost like an immortal jellyfish birthing itself over and over.

But in this room, this inescapable room, I come face to face with the Witch.

— . —

From Kentucky bluegrass and ginseng and wild rye to rhubarb and broccoli and kohlrabi; from sassafras and American pawpaw and red mulberry to cherry and Juneberry and blackberry bramble; my grandmother journeys from the tobacco fields of Kentucky and the poverty of Appalachia to find work as a janitor at Boys Town, formerly Father Flanagan's Boys' Home, formerly the City of Little Men.

Origin stories of Boys Town—ones that are decidedly less earthy than my grandmother's ghost garden—populate the area like crabgrass, their alacrity vomited out in equal parts hushed allegations and apologetics.

A boy named Howard Loomis was allegedly abandoned there, as the story goes, told as if his mother were a witch or a monster rather than an unmarried woman at the turn of the century struggling to care for her son, who was disabled from polio. "She abandoned her own son," Midwesterners say in coffee shops and in the local paper, the haunting of a woman who must make hard choices still gripping the populace one hundred years later. Like a Norman Rockwell re-creation of something a bit more sinister, a bronze statue of Howard now peers over the prairie.

As the story goes, older boys at the City of Little Men carried Howard around on account of his braced legs. Father Flanagan allegedly asked Reuben Granger, an older boy, if carrying Howard was difficult.

Reuben replied, "He ain't heavy, Father . . . he's m' brother." And so a jovial fantasy was born like a fire-heated mark on a branded cow. The statement graces the bottom of the bronze statue and every other form of fucking propaganda in this town, this cherished myth of originality that was, actually, stolen from an image in *Ideals* magazine. In the magazine, which predates the Boys Town brand, an older boy carrying a younger one is captioned, "He ain't heavy, mister . . . he's my brother."

The statue—and an ornate, vaulted church with the marble-sheathed tomb of Father Flanagan—is all that's left in the spaces where my grandmother's garden once grew. Her Three Sisters are now covered in concrete to make way for car dealerships and office buildings that will eventually rot with neglect during the global pandemic.

My grandmother doesn't even come up in a Google search on the history of Boys Town, her soil-loving sacrifices to the goddesses of nature washed away in the storm of stories about witchy women and helpful little boys.

No wonder she haunts the place.

— · —

The veil of sulfate blots out the sun (not that I could see it, anyway). The Witch holds me on the cast-iron bed with the horsehair mattress like she knows what's about to happen to me, like it's happened to her before. She croons in a dubious effort to assuage my anxieties, the way she does when I later give birth to a baby that is not breathing. My body is lifted off the bed by an evil force, a force that hates women, and it breaks me.

I am a wretch in the air, my limbs agitated as if shocked by electricity, and my bones snapping by way of coerced contortion.

When I awake in paroxysmal paralysis to the sound of my own screams, my blood congealed with horror, I find that my dead grandmother is at my side, all yellow-eyed and patchwork flesh.

I tell her that it's okay; I tell her that *we* are okay. She turns the color of parsnip and then a mare's tail, and floats away.

While we both hoped our outward appearances as fallible women might be pardoned, I know that we are contented, instead, to catalog our sins and to be monsters together in the absence of virtue.

I close my eyes and pray to the void.

Andi . . . .

She is hard to love, sometimes. And when I tell her as much, she tells me to "get fucked."

Her right eye is shot in the streets of LA and she is arrested several times for meth. My child will later call her "Aunt Andi with One Eye."

The first time I meet her, she asks if I'll go dumpster diving in the rich suburbs of Las Vegas; I tell her that I need to masturbate instead because I am too afraid. I also want her to think that I'm edgy.

Later, when I am assaulted by my partner, I will text only her. And she will respond: "Get your finances in order."

That's it. Just "get your finances in order."

When she is pregnant, she buys an iron Medusa head with snakes spinning in the air. "For the nursery," she texts.

And then she miscarries.

When her father dies during the COVID pandemic, I send her bags and bags of coffee. She and her mother sip the stuff in the darkening desert eventide over the dead body.

I miss holding her hand. I miss nuzzling the soft spaces of her neck and I miss the way she speaks Greek when she doesn't want me to know that she's talking shit.

2007, 22 years old

Dear Gillian,

Here I am, at 12:07 in the morning, in a motel room in Iowa.

I am alone. Alone with my smokes, an empty condom box, a half-smoked cigar, and of course, my journal. As well as a stack of 100-dollar bills. Five of them, actually. I finally answered Dennis's phone calls and I am officially a hooker. Ha! I feel amazing and ALIVE!

We talked politics and talked about society and communism.

Dennis thinks I'm smart. He's had many whores, one of which cried immediately after fucking him. He's so great, a fun fuck, and insists on protection—what's to cry about?

He took two showers, dressed, and said the room was mine for the remainder of the evening.

"Invite your friends!" he said.

So Marita is coming to spend the night with me.

I love women so damn much.

10. Other Timelines

The musk is rather piquant, just as it was in my youth. We used to smoke cigarettes inside the walls of the place's cool, exposed brick, our stripling palms clasping plastic ashtrays while reading *The Communist Manifesto* and shelling out lunch monies for Dashboard Confessional vinyls.

Now you have to smoke outside.

The trees are just starting their emergence back into the world of the living; the catalpa unlaces efflorescent leaves a bit slower, like a striptease, the margins taking weeks longer than most to unfurl from the midrib. Purple blankets drape the prairie in the promises of spring.

The bookstore is a kind of hoarder's paradise—crooked stacks of books reach the vaulted ceilings, organized imprecisely by subject matter. Hank Williams records slide out of their sleeves, threatening to disappear behind half-drunk Styrofoam cups of coffee and metal boxes with old-style organizing tabs. Dusty first editions present themselves like a cavalcade behind clouded glass, and velvet couches spit up soot when you sit on them.

The book buyer is a woman I know from the bar. She never remembers me, though, and often stumbles over the cobblestone labyrinths of our increasingly gentrified downtown.

Her glasses fall off her nose and she shoves them back up again in between puffs of cigarette smoke and sips of vodka.

She falls in bed with the bartender, himself aged with that particular masculine cadence of unfiltered cigarettes and yet still young enough to be her son. This makes me like them both exponentially more.

I bump into them in the servants' stairwell of a late nineteenth-century mansion, clumsily converted to apartments, of which the bartender occupies the central air–less attic. The book buyer is drunk then, nearly a decade before I peddle off my *Lolita* to her. I am exiting a threesome on the third floor of the mansion after a foolhardy musician asks me to fist his asshole the way I fist my girlfriend.

— . —

"I'd like to sell this," I say to the book buyer.

I show her my first-edition *Lolita*. Still in good shape with its original dust jacket from 1955.

"American, though," she says, examining it.

I am already overdrawn six dollars and some change for the month.

"Why do you want to part with it?" she asks, keeping time by flicking her eyes from the book to her shoes and back.

"I think I need to let go of her," I say, which is mostly true. The book buyer looks at *Lolita*, as if to ask, *Well, wuddaya say, ole girl?*

My brow weeps pearls of whiskey-soaked sweat.

— . —

I've developed a sour taste for attending AA meetings engorged with drink—it makes me friendlier, more open to the experience, I tell myself. I couldn't possibly get on my knees without a few cocktails.

A frosty-eyed, oyster-kind-of-a-man says, "I'm living proof that you can get sober and still be a piece of shit."

I hadn't thought of that comforting prospect.

Later, the Oyster Man texts me privately: "Stop with the bullshit and start telling the truth."

I contemplate texting back something about the ephemerality and porousness of truth but instead I quit AA altogether.

— · —

Tolstoy ends *War and Peace* (the second time) by contemplating *the question of history*, or rather, the problem of Truth. The truths of history, just like those of astronomy, must be constantly revised, he says. It is only through these fine-tuned revisions that we come to see history—and our place within it—as both interdependent and intersubjective. (When feminists argue as much, we are accused of "navel-gazing." But I digress.)

Compare this to Fitzgerald's watery ending to *The Great Gatsby*, in which Nick Carraway laments that we are all *borne back ceaselessly into the past*.

A fun paradox: the universe as both fatally deterministic and open to revisions.

Most of the time, I adhere to the philosophy that we are all constantly ping-ponged throughout all of time and space, throughout all timelines, in an endless and pointless game of whiff-whaff.

The truth is, it's easier to drink. I can pinpoint my addictions as if on a two-dimensional map, shrugging my shoulders and ducking all accountability. It's as if letting what I love kill me appeals to the siren song of an impartial universe. Most of the time, I act like my only purpose on this planet is to convince those in my unfortunate orbit that nothing matters.

The truth is, I let go of *Lolita* because I've always been willing to sell the parts of me that I can live without. I still pine for her, perhaps problematically, even months later. I want to be with her *over the timber claims and cow pastures, the corn belt, the cotton belt, [and] the cattle ranches*, to quote the poet Carl Sandburg in "Prairie"; I want to keep reading her, buoyed by the fantastic notion that her ending might change.

Perhaps, in another timeline, Humbert Humbert doesn't say to a pregnant Sally Horner, the real-life girlchild who was raped and tortured and on whom *Lolita* was based, *I hope you will love your baby. I hope it will be a boy.*

— · —

In Andy Weir's short story "The Egg," the character God says, *Once you've lived every human life throughout all time, you will have grown enough to be born.* I like this conception of endings best.

I am not as concerned as most about the implication that all of us are Hitler at some point in this equation of infinite refractions. Instead, I am drawn closer to my child—sweet milky breath, cradling kittens in barnyards, watching Brian

Greene on YouTube with lippy smears of strawberry popsicle. And I think, in another timeline, my child is *me*.

This sobering realization strapped to my boot like a pistol, I decide, at least for today, to live long enough to be born.

I'm ready to see how much I can take.

Acknowledgments

I would like to acknowledge the radical and tireless work of the editors at *Tits and Sass*, the first publication to support my work. *Tits and Sass* is a national treasure. A huge thanks to Michelle Tea's *Mutha Magazine*, as well, for publishing some raw stuff of mine when I was in the throes of postpartum depression.

A special thank you to Jamia Wilson, who offered brilliant suggestions during the initial phases of this book, and to Nick Whitney, whose boundless creativity helped me complete it.

I am forever indebted to—and inspired by—the work and lives of legends like Marsha P. Johnson, Sylvia Rivera, and Miss Major. Trans women of color have always been at the helm of movements that give and sustain life, including the sex workers' rights movement.

I am forever indebted to the amazing sex workers I get to orbit with regularity. It breaks my heart that our culture's compulsion to stigmatize and criminalize you prevents me from naming you here; these are both the manifest and latent functions of whorephobia, I think. That is, to push you into the shadows where your names are scarcely spoken. It is a brutal system rooted in hate and I hope to be your continued accomplice as we dismantle it together.

And to my child, of course. My multiverse.

My everything.

JUNIPER FITZGERALD is a mother, former sex worker, and academic based in the Midwest. Her children's book, *How Mamas Love Their Babies*, was published by Feminist Press in 2018 and was the first to feature a sex-working parent. Beyond her scholarly work, she has contributed to *We Too: Essays on Sex Work and Survival*, and her writing has appeared in *Tits and Sass*, *MUTHA Magazine*, and the *Rumpus*. She holds a PhD in sociology and is a lifelong Gillian Anderson fan.